PRESENTED TO:

....

FROM:

....

DATE:

....

Our Heart ♡ His Mission

Daily devotions from

South Texas AG Women's Ministry

Special Appreciation

The STX Women wish to express our special appreciation to Melissa Kautz for her efforts in pulling this book together. She tirelessly organized, e-mailed, and contacted people to ensure every detail fell into place.

Debbi Audorff and Marcia Walden proofed the final draft. Their keen eyes winnowed the chaff (typos) from the wheat (submissions) and helped make this book the best it could be.

Thank you!!

Foreword

If you want something done in a mighty way, hand it to a motivated woman. This book, *Our Heart His Mission*, is evidence of that.

When my wife, Jill, shared her discussion with Laura Yarbrough about building a book of collected devotionals from the South Texas (STX) Women, I was thrilled. Then Covid-19 tried to derail the project, and at one point, it seemed it wouldn't come together. The nation and the world were shutting down. It didn't seem possible that even the STX Women could pull off a task that the devil was determined to kick to the wayside.

Yet, this book wasn't just Jill and Laura's project, and it wasn't just the STX Women's project. It was God's project, and when God places an idea in the hearts of determined women, they always find a way.

Read about the woman who touched the hem of Jesus' cloak. Jesus said to her, "Daughter, your faith has healed you."

Then there was Jesus' special compassion for

trusted friend. Each one will touch your emotions with inspirational and heartfelt revelations and Biblical insights of encouragement.

Add this book to your library and prepare yourself for a blessing! Get extra copies, because you will want to share this book with everyone you know.

Tim R. Barker, Superintendent
South Texas District of the Assemblies of God
March 2021

Introduction

Our Heart His Mission is a collaboration (something women are good at) between Laura Yarbrough, myself, and the women of the South Texas Assemblies of God.

Laura put the bug in my ear, and when I spoke to my husband, Tim, he was immediately onboard. Then came Covid-19 to challenge our plans to bring this book into print.

Closures. Quarantines. Working from home. We missed the connection of Sunday mornings, weekly outings, and shared experiences with our families and friends.

Yet, if 2020 taught us anything, it was to step back and evaluate our lives. Staying home and quarantining made us realize just how special our time together in Jesus really is. Our dream for this book didn't fade. It became more vital than before.

It was an opportunity for God to speak a Word of power over the challenges we faced. We needed to break through the roadblocks the devil was throwing against us. One of those breakthroughs came in

Contributors

Debbi Audorff is an AGUSM Missionary with AGORA Ministries, an inner-city ministry in San Antonio. She and her husband Roger are also the STX District Missions Directors. She makes her home in Schertz. *("Sometimes It's Difficult to Love," p 170)*

Jill Barker is the STX Women's Ministries Director and the wife of STX Superintendent Tim Barker. She lives in Houston. *("Little Foxes," p 112)*

Kelly Baumgartner is an AGUSM Missionary serving in Intercultural Ministries. She lives in New Braunfels. *("Soldier, Athlete, Farmer," p 136)*

Rachel Chima is the Outreach Pastor at Legacy Church in Stafford. Rachel makes her home in Houston. *("Unbothered," p 141)*

Sherri Davila serves as Associate Pastor and is a Pastor's Wife at First Assembly in Pearsall. She is not only a Soccer Mom, she homeschools her 16-year-old son, Joshua. She resides in Pearsall. *("It's on the Inside of You," p 176)*

Heather Fallis is an AGWM Missionary currently serving in a Sensitive Area. Her spiritual home is Houston. *("Living Out God's Will," p 123)*

Medina Ford is a Pastor's Wife and Co-Pastors at New Song Fellowship. She calls Houston home. *("Does God Really Love Me?" p 36; "God Is the God that Sees Me," p 79)*

Our Heart His Mission

Porte home. ("When the Attacker Was Inside the House," p 57; "It's Time to Move," p 181)

Melissa LeClare is the STX Girls Ministries Director. She calls Houston home. ("Permission and Perspective," p 1; "There Is Power in Your Perspective," p 51; "In the In-between," p 90)

Suellyn Melder is the Missions Coordinator, Girls High School Teacher and Church Office Secretary at Old River Assembly of God in Dayton. She makes her home in Dayton. Follow Suellyn at her blog, www.justbreadcrumbs.com. ("Beloved," p 13)

Deborah Prihoda is the Houston Section Presbyter and the Lead Pastor at Embassy Church in Rosenberg. She sets her roots in Houston. ("Growing Through Trials," p 166)

Laura Romero is the STX Women's Ministries Administrator. She lives in Houston. ("Well Rested," p 84)

Terri Sparks is the Administrative Pastor at Encounter Church in Groves. She makes her home in Groves. ("Change What You SAY," p 117)

Sydney Strawn is a Campus Missionary at A&M, Prairie View Campus, with Chi Alpha. She calls Prairie View home. ("Surrender," p 65)

Dolly Thomas, Ph.D. is with Adult & Teen Challenge of Texas and serves the women of Houston. She makes her home in Alvin. ("Choose Maranatha," p 132)

Teri VanSelous is a Worship Team member at First Assembly of God, La Porte. She makes her home in La Porte. ("Beautifully Broken," p 7; "Above All the Noise," p 73)

Our Heart His Mission

Contents

Our Heart His Mission

Permission and Perspective

MELISSA LECLARE – HOUSTON, TEXAS

Your position will affect your perspective. Don't believe me? Have you ever taught a teenager to drive? There is a big difference in your perspective from the driver's seat to the passenger's seat. What might be 6-8 inches might as well be 6-8 feet. I can't be the only mom who has ever tried to move the car over to the left 12 inches just by leaning to the left. When you're sitting on the passenger side teaching your teen, the cars—or in the case of Houston, the barricades—seem a lot closer to the side of the car. How many have ever tried to slow the car down

Our Heart His Mission

In Mark 5 we read the story of four friends that carried their paralyzed friend to see Jesus. They knew that one encounter with Jesus would change everything. What they saw with their natural eyes seemed impossible. They could have said, "Sorry, brother, but we tried. I guess today isn't your day. We will try again another time." But they weren't satisfied with that.

They knew with a little extra effort and some hard work, they could get their friend to Jesus. They had the faith to say that if their friend could just get to Jesus, his life would be changed forever. So, they changed their position to affect their perspective. They chose to rise above what they saw with their natural eyes and carried their friend up to the roof. They cut a hole in the roof, lowered their friend down, and Jesus not only healed him but forgave his sins. They changed their position to change their perspective.

The Woman with an Issue of Blood

In Matthew 9 we read the story of the woman with an issue of blood. She was desperate to see and feeling the effects of Covid-19, what we saw with our natural eyes was that ministry looked impossible. How could we minister to our churches if we couldn't even get in the building? How could we minister to our children if we couldn't be with them? Limitations were placed on us that were beyond our control.

The church knew that we still needed to encounter Jesus. Our children still needed a time with Jesus. What we saw with our natural eyes seemed impossible, but we rose up and said, "With a little extra effort and hard work, we will still see Jesus." So, the church changed its position to change its perspective.

No longer were pastors standing in front of their congregations or youth and children's pastors meeting with their kids for an hour on Wednesdays. Now we were learning Zoom, Google Classroom, and how to livestream. We were making videos of children's lessons and dropping off activity packets for the children's ministries. Why? Because we knew that one encounter with Jesus could still change a person's life!

Beautifully Broken

TERI VANSELOUS – LA PORTE, TEXAS

Sitting at my desk, tears streaming down my face, my heart racing in my chest, I remember thinking: I don't know what's happening to me; nothing makes sense right now!

My day had started off well enough. I felt an atypical confidence in my plans, and the drive to work was decent. But, something changed when I pulled into the parking space. It wasn't drastic or immediately recognizable, just a slight sense of dread. Pushing it aside, I entered the building and started my workday routine. It wasn't until I set out on the long walk from my classroom to the faculty realized—this required professional attention.

Two weeks later, I sat in the doctor's office recounting my episode with great trepidation. Then, after listening very closely and intently to the picture that I hoped I painted for him, the doctor asked me two questions: Had I ever experienced anything like this before, and had I ever thought about killing myself?

The first answer came easily. "No, I've never experienced anything like this before."

The second was more complicated. I had never considered suicide, but I had questioned whether or not everyone around me would be better off without the burden of me in their lives. I'd even gone as far as contemplating what it would be like to move to another state, somewhere no one knew me and I could start over, without anyone else knowing.

"What is wrong with me?" I pleaded, tears wetting my eyes, a lump in my throat. Seeing my distress, the doctor quickly reassured me, explaining that I was experiencing classic symptoms of depression and anxiety; what I had described to him was nothing more than a panic attack.

come, they were quiet reminders of the brokenness and shame carried by people in the Bible. People like Rahab, King David, Ruth, the woman at the well, the woman with the issue of blood, and especially the sinful woman that anointed Jesus' feet in Luke 7:36-50.

As I reflected on each person and their story, I started to recognize the one thing they all had in common: despite their brokenness, God used them for His beautiful and glorious purpose. Each person was used by God to demonstrate His steadfast love.

In the time that's passed since my panic attack, I've learned a lot about myself, especially my faith and dependence on God. I've also spent a lot of time in prayer and Bible study to help me see myself through God's eyes rather than listening to the negative voices that contradict what His Word says. But, the greatest knowledge I've gained through this journey is that God often does His best works through the most broken people.

Although there are days I still struggle with the heaviness of depression and anxiety, I no longer feel the same sense of shame. Instead, I simply allow

Beloved

SUELLYN MELDER – DAYTON, TEXAS

I am my beloved's and my beloved is mine ...

Song of Solomon 6:3

Song of Solomon is an allegorical story of two lovers, a king and His Shulamite. She has little to offer and He is grand in every respect, *"outstanding among ten thousand"* (S. of S. 5:10). Yet, she sings with such contentment that she is all His and He is hers. Their love is anchored with this word of endearment, "beloved." I had to look it up.

It turns out the word beloved in Hebrew is dodi.

the Shulamite, I sing with gusto, "His desire is for me!" And of course, you, too.

Need more proof? Revelation 4 gives us a glimpse at the throne room. As the twenty-four elders lay down their crowns, they say something that gives us a glimpse of God's view of creation.

Thou art worthy, O Lord, to receive glory and honor and power; for Thou hast created all things, and for thy pleasure they are and were created.

Revelation 4:11

You see? You and I were created by God for His pleasure. He enjoys you and me. Think about your own children. You fell in love even before their first cry. My son has been my pleasure all his days. Has every day been a picture of obedience? No. Every homeschooling lesson a beautiful exchange of questions and knowledge? HA! Not to mention potty training, monitoring social media, and eating vegetables. There have been hard seasons along the way.

to find the one where I might belong.

The first one I read is KNOWLEDGEABLE. Not exactly me. I can only wish as we pass by.

Next, WORK IN PROGRESS. Yep, that's where I belong. I prepare to sit when I feel the Lord tug my hand. Well, I thought I was progressing.

Next table, CHRISTIAN Class 2. Probably ... on a good day. The Lord continues to lead. This isn't my table, either. Evidently there is a Class 3 ... or 12.

I'm getting a little discouraged. We walk past WEAK WITNESS. Thankfully. Although I'm sure the Lord knew that was an apt description of the friend with whom He held hands.

Then I saw it. FORGIVEN. I immediately attempted to pull out a chair. I don't want to be noticed at the head of this table but am thankful it's true. The Lord pushed in the chair. It was not for me.

Nonplussed, I had to ask. "Lord, surely I am forgiven. Please let me sit here."

The Lord smiled and squeezed my hand. "Yes, you are forgiven, my daughter, but it is not for your sins that I know you. Come on."

We then passed the banner MUCH AFRAID and

Our Heart His Mission

because my banner over you is LOVE!"

Power Confession

I have a God who fights my battles for me.

*You shall not fear them; for Yahweh
your God himself fights for you.*

Deuteronomy 3:22

and enjoying the beautiful scenery around me, the Lord drew my attention to this rusty old chair that I walk by frequently.

It reminds me of what we look like when we allow ourselves to remain outside in the abusive elements of the storms of life around us, instead of allowing the Lord to bring us shelter, refuge and healing. We become just like this chair, hollow, empty, unable to function in the way we were created to function.

We become brittle, sharp, and dangerous to those who approach us. We crumble and perish under the elements that have been unleashed on us.

But Jesus has provided a refuge, a place of safety and healing if we will just allow Him to come in and take over. But we must turn—*meaning to turn around and totally change direction without sight of the new path.*

We know that and it sounds so beautiful, but it requires reconstruction which can be painful in the process. Yet, it will produce such a beautiful, useful product in the end.

For me, my role is laying down daily my will, my

⟨⟩ Power Confession ⟨⟩

I am filled with the strength and peace of God.

Yahweh will give strength to his people.
Yahweh will bless his people with peace.

Psalm 29:11

The definition of **commitment** is:

The state or quality of being dedicated to something.

I believe that when you truly commit to something, you say YES and you mean it. This yes is not limited to a certain time constraint either. We must be flexible and understand that with our "commitment" we also agreed to be flexible.

Let me give you an example. When we sign our boys up for baseball, they give us a schedule for practices and games. BUT when we have bad weather, like we often do here in Southeast Texas, we find that those "schedules" mean nothing. Is it frustrating? YES! I am OCD and love routine! Don't mess with my schedule. However, we agreed and committed that our boys would participate and be a part of a team. This means that we have to be flexible when the practices are moved across town because the field was too wet, or games are postponed for whatever reason.

Here is what I want to leave you with today…

God's Glory and Might

VALERIE WHITNEY – HOUSTON, TEXAS

Stars

The dazzling creatures of the Heavens.
Proclaiming God's Glory and Might.
He breathed them into this world; and just like
that, they lit up the Raven night.
Each one brings peace to the troubled hearts.
Letting each believer know, God is always here.
A living work of art, the stars He swirled into the
sky.
Like a stream of life, proclaiming His Glory and
Might.

Our Heart His Mission

His blood sacrifice calls me forgiven.
His love calls me home to His everlasting
    Kingdom of grace.
Lord, how can I comprehend your glory?
It is greater than the amount of stars that inhabit
    the night.
Your love shines brighter than the sun,
Like a vast array of unloving colors. Dazzling on
    the souls of all who occupy the earth.
Lord, your love chooses all.
Who can run from it?
Who can comprehend it?
Who can surmount it?
For your love is not of this earth, but it comes
    from a place Everlasting.

Glory

The reverence of the Lord
His Sovereignty reigns on high
Glory unto Him
Until the day of Ezekiel

of mountaintops
The angels' trumpets sing
Of glorious splendor to their Mighty King
King of Kings
Holy of Holies
You will reign
For all eternity.

Power Confession

I find peace and rest in the shadow of the Almighty.

He who dwells in the secret place of the Most High will rest in the shadow of the Almighty.

Psalm 91:1

Nowadays I long for, even cling to, those exact words, but not exactly from the disciplining finger or choir loft stare ... now it is an entirely different meaning. I want the gentle reminder, not the scolding "or else" one. Be still. I want to read those words, sing them, envelope myself with every verse in the Bible that contains those two powerful words.

Psalm 37:7 emphasizes quietness, waiting for the Lord and not worrying. Psalm 46:10 says simply, *"Be still and know that I am God."* Even in the midst of the storm, Jesus spoke, *"Peace, be still,"* to the wind and waves, and they became perfectly calm (Mark 4:39). In Exodus 14:14 it says that God will fight for us; we just need to be still.

Those two words mean so much from our Creator. He reminds us that He's "got this" ... whatever "it" may be in our lives. He reassures us that nothing is too big for Him to handle. He calms the storms; He is our protector; He teaches us trust. My mom had her reasons for wanting me to be still—whether it was to encourage active listening to the pastor or to be reminded that my behavior was a direct reflection of her parenting skills ... or maybe a little of both.

⤳ Power Confession ⤳

I am filled with hope through the power of the Spirit.

Hope doesn't disappoint us, because God's love has been poured out into our hearts through the Holy Spirit who was given to us.

Romans 5:5

allow those things to happen—not if he really loved me—not if he really loves my family.

What is so awesome about our loving God is that He understands our deepest hurts and sorrows and He comes to us with that answer and peace—if we only just ask Him and trust Him.

I have had a deep faith in my Lord Jesus Christ for many years and often wondered why anyone would even doubt His Love. Then there was a time that such "wrong" set in all around me and my family. I couldn't image that God really loved me if He allowed those circumstances to happen to me and to my family. So, I asked God about it.

It was a Sunday morning, and I was getting ready to go to church. I had been really hurting and was upset and crying. I looked straight in the mirror and talked to God as if He were at my side. I asked Him why He allowed those things to happen to me and my family. Then I looked straight at the mirror and said, "God, I don't believe that You love me. You don't love me. Why, God, did all this happen? You don't love me." Then I said to Him, "If you love me, show me." If I'm honest, I threw an item—I don't and yet he was following me all over the place that morning telling me that God loved me. At the end of the service, after the altar call, I had just finished praying with some people and that same man walked up to me and once again, all he said was, "God loves you."

To be honest with you, it seemed like he overdid it that morning. He came up to me about a dozen times to tell me that God loves me. Then, as the building was almost empty, once more, that same man came up to me and said, "God loves you." Then we all left and went home.

The next Sunday when I saw him, it was just a normal hello and greeting from that same man. He will never know why he did that that day, as I didn't see him much after that time.

But God knew. GOD DID CARE ABOUT ME and he used an ordinary man to remind me of that. I hang on to God's promises when I get discouraged, and I know that He is the God that does care for me and loves me. You know what, He cares about you and loves you, too.

Called. Equipped. Qualified.

APRIL JONES – MCALLEN, TEXAS

*Remember, dear brothers and sisters, that
few of you were wise in the world's eyes or
powerful or wealthy when God called you.
Instead, God chose things the world
considers foolish in order to shame those
who think they are wise. And he chose things
that are powerless to shame those who are
powerful.*

1 Corinthians 1:26-27 (NLT)

We've all heard the phrase, He doesn't call the

from time to time. What I am saying is that you are called by God and you have already been given everything you need to fulfill your God-given commission. Because HIS strength is perfect!

What a liberating revelation!

All you need is a willingness to follow Him and do your part, because He is actively and perfectly doing His part.

I'm also not implying that the thing you're going through right now is not hard or difficult. What I am clarifying is that even in the midst of your storm (or I guess I should say, *especially* in the midst of your storm), He wants to show Himself faithful in your life so that a confused, lost and dying world can see a little bit of His glory through your frail and imperfect life.

Remember, even Jesus implored of His Father:

My Father! If it is possible, let this cup of suffering be taken away from me. Yet I want your will to be done, not mine.

Matthew 26:39

⊰⊱ Power Confession ⊰⊱

I am followed by the signs and wonders of the power of Jesus.

In the power of signs and wonders, in the power of God's Spirit; so that from Jerusalem, and around as far as to Illyricum, I have fully preached the Good News of Christ.

Romans 15:19

and my personal time with God. When, God? Why, God? (I'm sure I used the other three ... Where, What and How.) As I was making Izzy's bed, God took out His highlighter on me ... He gave me a revelation ... as I had been asking these questions, He had been answering by giving me His peace and reminding of His promises through His Word! Scriptures like:

Be alert and of sober mind. Your enemy the devil prowls around like a roaring lion looking for someone to devour. Resist him, standing firm in the faith, because you know that the family of believers throughout the world is undergoing the same kind of sufferings. And the God of all grace, who called you to his eternal glory in Christ, after you have suffered a little while, will himself restore you and make you strong, firm and steadfast.

1 Peter 5:8-10

Above all else, guard your heart, for

I realized these words build and set a frame of time into motion, and I am the architect building this exact timeframe! When I build this limited time-frame, I instantly feel stress and frustration, like I'm staring down the road of never!

But as I've been asking these time-reference questions, God, through His loving, daily reminders, has been going down the list with me, helping me to cross the words (questions) off my list; never failing to provide the answer ... peace ... be watchful ... be expecting ... I am with you.

It's okay to ask these daring questions, as long as we do not allow them to imprison us. Instead, may we use them to position us to keep us centered on our Heavenly Father and His Word that will never fail us. When we feel that we can't find the next word on that crossword puzzle list, let's give God room to highlight it for us. He is faithful like that!

There Is Power in Your Perspective

MELISSA LECLARE – HOUSTON, TEXAS

I have a very active imagination. My dreams are often detailed and eventful. Most of the time I remember them, but they really have no purpose or impact. There have been dreams, while few and far between, that I have woken from and jotted some thoughts down because of how it spoke to me. Let me share with you the latest dream I had and the lesson it taught me.

In my dream, we had just finished the new district ministries center and it was move-in day. Everyone was excited as we were all setting up our the side and said very sincerely, "I'm sorry we had to put your office in the bathroom. It's the only space we had available."

In my mind, I thought, wait, my office is in the bathroom?! but I said, "Wow, perspective is everything." He saw my office in the bathroom. I saw that I had a bathroom in my office.

Our perspective will determine how we act and react to situations. There is an old anecdote that tells the story of two successful shoe salesmen that go to a remote part of Africa to sell shoes.

After three days, the first man says, "I want to return home. Get me out of here. This is useless. Nobody over here wears shoes."

The second man calls home and says, "Send me everything we have. This is awesome. Nobody over here wears shoes!"

The difference is the power of perspective.

I think the best story in the Bible about the power of perspective is David and Goliath. The Israelites saw Goliath as someone too big to fight. David saw him as someone too big to miss.

The most important decision you can make on a

PERSPECTIVE!

What's your self-talk like? Do you say, I can't do this, I don't know what I'm doing, I'm not good at this OR do you say by the power and spirit of the living God working inside of me, I am bold, confident, and able!

If you can't see it with your eyes today, speak it by faith for tomorrow. Proper perspective sees problems as possibilities.

We are all faced with a series of great opportunities brilliantly disguised as impossible situations.

— Chuck Swindoll —

There is power in your perspective.

When the Attacker Was Inside the House

STEPHANIE KELLER – LA PORTE, TEXAS

The words that Jesus had just spoken hung in the air, making it thick with tension and difficult to breathe. "One of you will betray me."

Matthew 26 tells us that Jesus answered Judas when he asked, "Surely, not I, Lord," with, "Yes, it is you." But in John 16 it says that Jesus told all the disciples that the one who would betray Him was the one to whom He would pass a piece of bread. Then handing it to Judas, Judas fled into the night. Either way, His point was made.

Later on, we read that Jesus was brought before

right hand of the Pharaoh and saved numerous groups of people in and around Egypt, including his family. But, still, it was his family, his brothers that sold him.

Why tell the less glorious side of these two stories? Because I think we need to spend a little time admitting that when tough times come, we certainly struggle, but when the blow comes from inside the House of God, it lands harder and hurts worse. We tend to put on our pretty church face a few times a week and act like everything is perfect and nothing ever goes wrong. After all, we don't want to scare the lost away and keep them from coming to Christ.

I am not supporting the idea of airing dirty laundry in public, but I do think we need to acknowledge that it happens; and the fact that we don't face it is. keeping some of us in bondage to that hurt for far too long. It's time we stopped putting on the pretty church face and started "coming as we are." Even as believers who have already "walked" the Roman Road and been baptized in water, we don't stand on a mountain and shout praises for the rest of our lives.

have been a favorite weapon of the enemy against God's people as long as there has been a church (or a "chosen people of God" as it was in the Old Testament). Division is one of the greatest desires of the enemy because UNITY is the very heart of God. He seeks to destroy all that God ordained *"for the good of those who love him, who have been called according to his purpose."* (Rom. 8:28) Unity with other imperfect people in the family of God is one of His greatest plans for our good!

This is not to say that your situation is not unique. I have found that no matter how much I think my situation has in common with anyone else's, I cannot honestly say, "I know how you feel." Even if their case mirrors mine exactly outwardly, we have different pasts, different perspectives and we are different people. The beauty of it is that Jesus can say, "I know how you feel," because He is feeling it right along with you. You are seen, known and loved truly and completely by the only One who is capable of such knowledge and love. He is both, the High and Holy King of the universe and your closest friend, one who knows all your deepest secrets and but to those watching, your weakness cannot be seen at all, only His strength.

3. Go back.

If you left church, go back. If you stopped reading your Bible, start again. If you stopped working in a particular ministry, go back. If you turned in your ministry credentials, go back and get them.

When you go back, it won't be the same. That's OK. You're not the same. There may be some work that has to be done. Do it.

Open up. Ask God to heal you and help you to forgive. Forgiveness is not an instantaneous thing, but it is a process worth working through. It's also often a long one. Don't wait until you feel your forgiveness is complete to go back. Go back now. Work through the process there.

You are returning wiser, probably older, stronger and relying on God. Do not allow yourself to return angry, arrogant, vengeful or critical. Don't erect walls against further hurt. Open your heart to God and trust Him that He is writing a story in which you have a major part. No matter where the narrative

Surrender

SYDNEY STRAWN – PRAIRIE VIEW, TEXAS

Like a lot of women in America, I love Beyonce! Actually ... I loved Beyonce.

I enjoyed the artistic ability she possessed. I grew up listening to her, bought all her albums and concert performances, and played her album *B-Day* on repeat as my sister, cousin and I would dance in the living room, imitating her. We would put on a whole concert in the living room during the long summer months of my youth. I knew all her songs, and I especially loved her as a performer, specifically her dancing skills.

Around 2013, though, the music Beyonce put out

God working though this with me gave me a different view on surrender. Before I experienced this, I would have categorized surrender as a moment where I realize that God's understanding is infinite and mine is severely lacking and therefore I surrender what I think or want to do for what God is asking of me. Momentarily I'm devastated, perhaps crying at the altar, even wrestling with God, but in a few days' time, what I surrendered doesn't really leave a defining mark on my life. I move on, actually glad that I've surrendered that particular thing to the Lord, because deep down I actually agreed with Him.

Many of us are likely the same. We sometimes surrender to God because subconsciously we see that He is right, and what He is asking us to do makes sense.

But what about when we don't agree? Like my playlists? When what God is asking of us doesn't seem to make sense?

Do we surrender because God asks us to—or wait until we come to a place of better understanding of why God wants us to surrender something?

than what you can imagine.

But I wanted you to know brethren that the things which happened to me have actually turned out for the furtherance of the gospel. So that it has become evident to the whole palace guard, and to all the rest, that my chains are in Christ.

Philippians 1:12-13

Power Confession

I am filled with the courage of Christ in all situations.

... Draw near today to battle against your enemies. Don't let your heart faint! Don't be afraid, nor tremble, neither be scared of them.

Deuteronomy 20:3

dead in the eyes and said, "You have a problem saying no, my friend, and it is going to cost you." Reality was that it was already costing me my time and energy, but those things I mentioned earlier (family, marriage, sanity, health) were not for sale!

I am so thankful for this friend!! We all need people in our lives that speak TRUTH to us especially when we can't see it ourselves.

Listen, you guys, I am still not great at this and still spread myself too thin. What I did learn was that if it was going to cost me in areas that were not up for sale, then it's a no from me!

Some things are just not for sale. Say NO. Protect those things.

Peace I leave with you; my peace I give you. I do not give to you as the world gives. Do not let your hearts be troubled and do not be afraid.

John 14:27

Above All the Noise

TERI VANSELOUS – LA PORTE, TEXAS

My son, Erin, has always been a prolific eater, rarely turning down a meal. As a 5'10" and almost 180-pound, 13-year-old young man, mealtime is probably his favorite part of the day. This is especially true when it comes to holidays and family gatherings. He looks forward to Thanksgiving and the wide array of desserts that different family members bring to the buffet-style meal the most.

One of my favorite Thanksgiving memories of Erin occurred when he was about six or seven years old. The family planned an early dinner that year to help accommodate some conflicts in schedules, so face to face. He looked up at me and, with every ounce of his youthful innocence, asked, "Didn't you say something about chocolate?"

The room erupted with laughter.

I often find myself looking back at this memory and thinking about how much it reveals Erin's love of chocolate. But recently, God has used this memory to teach me a lesson about waiting and hearing His voice.

Erin could have gone against our will and snuck a snack or eaten too much before dinner, but the reward for his obedience was getting to enjoy all the foods and chocolate desserts his little tummy could hold, satisfying both his hunger pangs and his chocoholic heart. By allowing God to guide me and prepare my path, God will meet my needs, and my hunger pangs, whether spiritual, physical, financial, or emotional, will be satisfied. (Phil. 4:19)

Just like I knew that Erin was hungry and repeatedly asked him to be patient, promising him that it would all be worth it when the time came, God knows the desires of my heart—what I'm hungry for; more importantly, my immediate needs—and asks carrying on conversations at the front of the house that day, and I wasn't the only one that had talked about chocolate. Even though Erin's hunger dominated his mind, he also knew that he needed to wait and listen for me to let him know when it was time to eat. Over all the other noise in the house, he heard the voice he anticipated begin talking about the one thing his heart desired the most and came running.

Through this memory, God showed me that He wants me to listen for His voice above all the other noise that surrounds me and come running when He calls the same way that Erin did. Those noises aren't just audible sounds—they include all the obligations, responsibilities, and distractions I have as a wife, mother, daughter, sister, worship team member, teacher, and every other title that I carry.

God knows exactly what I need and when I need it and will meet those needs gladly. I just have to wait and listen for Him to guide me down the path that He has prepared for me.

God Is the God that Sees Me

MEDINA FORD – HOUSTON, TEXAS

Being involved in leadership in the ministry is very rewarding but can also be tough at times. Unfortunately, even when we are working hard and doing our best to serve God and serve others, there will be people who are critical of us. This happened with Jesus[1] and other Biblical people[2], but still we are shocked when it happens to us. Especially when it is often those who we are close to that hurt us.

---

[1] Jesus when healing a man's withered hand on the Sabbath
[2] Moses even after he helped the children of Israel cross the Red Sea

asked me (knowing the answer), wasn't it three miscarriages that you had? She continued describing the dream. My two sons, Wes (the oldest), then Kendall and my daughter Davita were upstairs in our game room playing pool. However, there were three more boys (young men) in the room as well. One was about a year older than Wes, and the other seemed to be only a few months older than Wes. The third boy was just months older than my second son, Kendall. They played pool and laughed together, then they commented to each other that they had better clean up so Mom doesn't get upset because "she might not let us go to the concert tonight."

As the details unfolded, I began to cry as my precious daughter-in-law Cristina went on with the details. She was being very open and vulnerable with me as she had never had dreams like that before. In a way that only the Lord God Almighty could do, the exact details begin to unfold of three miscarriages I had had in my earlier years of marriage. The ages of the young men she described matched the timeline and approximate age that the children I had carried for only a few short weeks each would have been,

---

⌒☙⌒ Power Confession ⌒☙⌒

I stand on the everlasting Rock, and I will trust in Him forever.

Trust in Yahweh forever; for in Yahweh is an everlasting Rock.

Isaiah 26:4

where you unwind, refresh, and move forward! We tend to schedule manis and pedis after a huge work project or hard week at the office, our remedy to ease our mental and physical states— "Us" drama queens call this act Tender. Love. Care! **There is absolutely nothing wrong with taking care of ourselves—in fact, it's necessary!** We need it to push forward. Without it we are angrier than our Hangry state (who knew that was possible)?!!! Well, maybe that's just me. But what if I told you the refreshment of your physical and mental state is a complementary by-product of your personal Spiritual wellness founded in the Word!

For I have given rest to the weary and joy to the sorrowing.

Jeremiah 31:25 (NLT)

Rest is much needed in the business of everyday life ... kids ... work ... school ... you name it! We need rest. In addition to rest, we need our Redeemer! He is our REST! I find comfort and peace that is *its leaf will not wither, and whatever he does will prosper.*

Psalms 1:2-3 (MEV)

The Bible is so completely nourishing; the closer we grow to God, the more we are nourished! We receive a Spiritual refreshment when we draw closer to Him, much like when drinking water to quench thirst. You'll prosper wherever you go and, through your shortcomings, you'll experience the peace of God that surpasses all understanding! Find rest in Him and the rest will fall into place—it may not be easy, but His love and peace are captivating!

The beauty in a woman is not in the clothes she wears, the figure that she carries, or the way she combs her hair. The beauty of a woman is seen in her eyes, because that is the doorway to her heart; the place where love resides. True beauty in a woman is reflected in her soul. It's the caring and that she lovingly gives the passion that she shows

---

Power Confession

I am wise through faith and filled with the power of God.

Your faith [stands not] in the wisdom of men, but in the power of God.

1 Corinthians 2:5

heart and mind. I thought, well, I know what that means, but what does it mean right now? A couple of hours down the road and I still wasn't getting anything to accompany the phrase. The hours passed. My music was thumping, snacks were being eaten, and still nothing. There came a moment during the trip that I literally said out loud, "God, I will be there in less than three hours. What do you mean by 'in the in-between'?"

As I was driving, listening to Kirk Franklin's station on the radio, all of a sudden the music drastically changed. It went from upbeat and rockin' to a mellow, slower worship song. It was such a change that it caught my attention and I glanced down to make sure I hadn't hit something to change the music channel. I noticed the title of the song, *Patiently Praising.*

Now, before you get the idea that I'm super spiritual when I travel, please know that before Kirk Franklin's station, I was listening to 70's classic rock, before that was Broadway hits, before that was southern gospel and I started the day off with country. Yes, I like a variety of music. It all depends be for healing, a job for someone, provision, direction, or salvation for a loved one. Some of us are further along in the in-between. My husband and I have been praying for over 23 years for the salvation of his parents. We haven't seen the answer yet. I believe we will, but until then, while we are in the in-between, may I be found faithful, joyful, loving God and serving others, and patiently praising for the answer that's to come.

Be encouraged of this today. No matter what you are facing, God hears, God knows, and He will be faithful to answer in His timing and His way. Be confident of this:

And we know [We don't have to wonder or guess for we KNOW!] that in all things God works for the good of those who love him, who have been called according to his purpose.

Romans 8:28 (NIV)

Beware of Thorns

SHAENELLE JOHNSTON – HOUSTON, TEXAS

The Parable of the Sower

*"Listen! Behold, a sower went out to sow.
And as he sowed, some seed fell along the
path, and the birds came and devoured it.
Other seed fell on rocky ground, where it did
not have much soil, and immediately it
sprang up, since it had no depth of soil. And
when the sun rose, it was scorched, and
since it had no root, it withered away. Other
seed fell among thorns, and the thorns grew
up and choked it, and it yielded no grain.*

In the last line we see that these seeds sprouted and grew! The plant was produced, as intended, but something got in the way of it reaching its full purpose. Thorns. These thorns grew right alongside the plant. As this crop began to flourish, so did the thorns. Eventually, the thorns overpowered the plant and brought its destiny of producing grain to an end.

Later in Mark 4, Jesus is explaining this parable to the disciples. He tells them that the seeds that fell among the thorns are those who hear the Word but let things get in the way. Those things are the cares of the world, the deceitfulness of riches, and the desires for other things. Hearing the Word is the easy part. We read the Bible, listen attentively to the Sunday morning service, pay attention and participate in small groups, etc., but outside of that we let life distract us. We self-assign expectations that drive our decisions instead of being motivated by a desire to be obedient to God's Plan for our lives. We allow information from the internet and social media to define our value, self-worth, and beauty, which in turns shapes our expectations of ourselves

Power Confession

I receive the Word of God as His inviolate truth for my life.

Now these [Jews] were more noble than those in Thessalonica, in that they received the word with all readiness of the mind, examining the Scriptures daily to see whether these things were so.

Acts 17:11

home in time to begin preparing dinner so we would have just enough time to make it to church on time for our midweek service.

And then I heard it. That familiar exploding sound that accompanies a flat tire. And then to further confirm my suspicions, the van started shimmying violently and forcefully veering to the side of the road as if it had a mind of its own.

As I sat on the side of the road waiting for roadside assistance to arrive, I found myself internally escalating, as thoughts such as, "I don't have time for this!" and "Really? Are you kidding? Why me?" were swirling through my brain. Isn't it interesting how quickly our emotions can skyrocket when our carefully planned-out agendas are blatantly disregarded?

All nine fruits of the Spirits were long gone. No love. No joy. No peace. Patience? Uh, no. Kindness? Uh-uh. Goodness? Nope. Faithfulness? I wish. Gentleness? Not even close. Self-Control? Are you kidding me?

What if we begin to stop the madness and, with the Holy Spirit's help, retrain our brains to see each love of Jesus in a manner that doesn't turn people off is to ask, "Can I pray with you about something?" He explained that most everyone on the planet prays in some sort or fashion and it can seem compassionate and kind to offer such a gesture.

As the technician worked on my van tire, I engaged him in conversation to avoid the awkwardness of silence. I asked about his family and then he asked me the same. After exchanging a few pleasantries, I referenced his family and then asked if there was anything I could pray with him about. He stopped what he was doing, looked up at me and said, "Yes, actually. There is something you can pray with me about." He then told me about something that he and his wife were worried about regarding one of their children. As he finished working on my tire, I closed my eyes, reached out my hand toward him and began to pray aloud for God to intervene in his family situation. Tears streaming down his face, he stood up and had me sign the paperwork. I promised him I would continue to pray for him and his family, and I reminded him that today God made sure he knew how much He loves him.

You Are Not Without a Father

BOBBIE GARCIA – HALLETTSVILLE, TEXAS

*And I will ask the Father, and he will give
you another advocate to help you and be
with you forever— the Spirit of truth. The
world cannot accept him, because it neither
sees him nor knows him. But you know him,
for he lives with you and will be in you. I will
not leave you as orphans; I will come to you.*

John 14:16-18

The Spirit you received does not make you

us. It is this indwelling of His presence that reminds us that we are truly God's very own children.

You are not without a father. You have a Father who is safe, reliable, and all-powerful, and He gives us access to all we need.

A prayer to our Father:

Father, today I sit in Your presence as Your child, a child with a great inheritance. Forgive me for not seeing all that You have offered me as a father. Comfort me with Your Holy Spirit who reminds me that I have a Father I can run to.

ᏼᏟ᠍ Power Confession ᠌ᏚᎧ

I am free from sin and death.

For the law of the Spirit of life in Christ Jesus made me free from the law of sin and of death.

Romans 8:2

some kind of flowering plant or fresh-cut flowers in my home.

When I worked with designing fresh flowers at a florist shop, I noticed that many beautiful flowers had no smell at all. Some flowers were very fragile and would bruise and crush very easily. There were also a couple types of flowers that were very strong and hearty that actually stank.

They looked beautiful but put your nose close to them and it was not a pleasant aroma at all!

But I especially remember a particular flower called Rubrum Lily also referred to as a Stargazer. When a shipment of Rubrum Lilies came in, everybody knew because the entire store would smell of their beautiful fragrance.

To this day if I walk in a store that carries fresh flowers and they have Rubrum Lilies in their bouquets, I immediately know because I recognize the smell.

It brings a flood of memories to me.

We leave a fragrance wherever we go. It can be an aroma of truth and love or it can be an aroma of stink. When we have been in the presence of Jesus

---

❧ Power Confession ❧

I am rooted in Christ and established in the faith.

[Be] rooted and built up in him, and established in the faith, even as you were taught, abounding in it in thanksgiving.

Colossians 2:7

Song of Songs 2:15 (KJV)

The scripture creates a picture of little foxes sneaking into the vineyards eating all the new growth or tender fruit. If that weren't enough, they would dig around the vine and branches destroying the branches. This sounds like my new little puppies digging and digging and digging.

Back to the foxes.

When you think of a little fox or see a picture of one you would probably say, "Aw, isn't he cute?" But if I ask what comes to mind when I say fox, I get many different answers: sneaky, sly, devil, cunning, and so on.

When I cross-referenced this passage, it took me to a study on John 15, *Study 5 – The Little Foxes that Spoil the Vines*, from the Words of Life Ministries by Rev. Francis W. Dixon.

Jesus refers to himself as the "vine." Believers are the "branches." If we stay connected to the source, Jesus, we will bear fruit.

Ok, now that makes sense why the "fox" would

What if the little fox has already entered the vineyard? We must kill it. I know that sounds awful. Remember, we are talking metaphorically.

Those who belong to Christ Jesus have crucified the flesh with its passions and desires.

Galatians 5:24

Get rid of the little foxes! They can and will grow up to become a BIG fox!

If we lose our fruit, we lose our witness.

No wonder my mother would tell me (often) that little foxes spoil the vine. She didn't want me to grow up with the "little" things in life becoming "big." If I could learn to conquer the things in life that would steal my joy, love, peace, patience, kindness, goodness, faithfulness, gentleness, and self-control (Gal. 5:22-23), then I would bear much fruit for Jesus!

Stay connected to the vine! Watch out for those foxes!!

Change What You SAY

TERRI SPARKS – GROVES, TEXAS

Years ago, if you had asked me what my heart's desire was for the local church, I would have answered, "To teach Christians how to live in victory!" You know what? I am STILL passionate about helping Christians live in victory! Whether you are in a leadership or pastoral role, or a faithful church attender, YOU CAN live in victory! Guess what, ladies! Even in the middle of an evil, chaotic world, you can live in victory! One way to make this happen is to make sure what you are saying lines up with what GOD is saying! Your words matter! Proverbs 13:3 tells us that *"He who guards his lips guards his* lives will change!

2. Words DETERMINE What You'll Have!

WORDS fuel results, one way or the other.

"For assuredly, I say to you, whoever says to this mountain, 'Be removed and be cast into the sea,' and does not doubt in his heart, but believes that those things he says will be done, he will have whatever he says."

Mark 11:23 (NKJV)

Basically, Mark 11:23 says, "You will have whatever you say."

Charles Capps said that the Lord told him this: "I have told my people that they can have what they say, and they are saying what they have."

So many times we come to God asking him for things that He has given us the ability to change—or make happen! He has given US the unique ability to set in motion things in our lives, by aligning our waver and receive at the same time. Satan wants to cause you to waver and doubt! But he can't do it without your cooperation. You are the only one who can give him access to your promises—and you do this through your words.

4. Speak GOD'S WORD!

The WORD OF GOD will CHANGE your circumstances as you SAY IT! And the more you MEDITATE on it, the more you will SAY it, and the more you will BELIEVE it!

There is only one way you can achieve this and do so for the long term—by meditating on the Word of God day and night (Joshua 1:8). This must become a lifestyle for us! Know the Word. Speak the Word.

HOW do I do this? Romans 10:17 – *"So then faith comes by hearing, and hearing by the word of God."*

Are you reading God's Word??? Your Bible??? Every day??? That's where you start! At some point, what you are reading is going to get into your heart. And then, whatever is in your heart is going to come out of your mouth! Luke 6:45 says, *"What you say*

Living Out God's Will

HEATHER FALLIS – HOUSTON, TEXAS

Since becoming a missionary, I can't tell you how many times I've heard people say, "You are heroes!" I wish I felt like a hero.

The reality is, most of the time the challenge of living in a foreign country, speaking a second language, and navigating ministry in the context of communism and persecution makes me feel like anything but. Some days it's all I can do to simply love my family and get dinner on the table. There's no superhero cape in my closet.

And yet, over and over again in the Scriptures, I am reminded that God isn't looking for people with

Why? Because we are incredibly dangerous to the kingdom of darkness when we know that we are overcomers and conquerors in Christ! We will rarely feel like the victorious and anointed women of God that He says we can be, but we must choose to live out of what we know rather than what we feel. We must be in the Word, filling our minds with the truth about who God says we can be in Him.

Gideon knew himself. He knew he was no hero. He knew that the odds were against the Israelites. So instead of throwing on a cape and jumping to action, he boldly voiced his concerns and doubts, admitting that it felt like the Lord had abandoned them. It didn't matter that he had been called a hero, all he could see was defeat.

Then the Lord turned to him and said,
"Go with the strength you have, and rescue
Israel from the Midianites. I am sending
you!"

Judges 6:14

Our Heart His Mission

When walking in God's calling on our lives, moments of doubt are inevitable. We are flawed, short-sighted people who often don't see the bigger picture of what God is doing in His people. So, it is abundantly good news for us that doubt doesn't disqualify us. But if our fragile faith isn't what qualifies us for God's call, what does? His presence. God's response to Gideon's doubt wasn't condemnation or exasperation. It was a reassurance of His presence with Gideon. A reminder that no matter how unqualified we feel for what God is asking of us, His presence is what equips, enables, and qualifies us to accomplish His will.

Five years into this life overseas and I am still learning to walk confidently in the calling that God has placed on my life. Even when I don't feel like a hero, even when I don't feel strong enough for the tasks before me, even when I doubt, my God is faithful to remind me that He is simply asking for my humble obedience. To believe I am who He says I am. To go in the strength I have and trust Him to do the rest. To abide in His presence because that is the only thing that qualifies me for this calling.

Dig Deep

Jordin Williams – Houston, Texas

When failure is not an option ...

I've heard it said, and so have you. "Failure is just not an option." I understand the notion, but if we aren't failing, are we even trying?

I can escape failing by just simply not trying. If you are failing ... CONGRATS!

You are living!

BUT there are truly times that failing is just not an option.

When are those times?

Raising our kids ...

Our Heart His Mission

My health ... *what's my WHY?*

Once you have established what it is that you cannot fail at and you know your WHY, you are much more likely to succeed in your journey.

Look to the LORD and his strength; seek his face always.

1 Chronicles 16:11

ᏻᏅᏋ Power Confession ᏋᏅᏻ

I am infused with wisdom, great power and strength in Christ.

A wise man has great power; and a knowledgeable man increases strength.

Proverbs 24:5

Christ, let him be Anathema Maranatha." Paul warned of the curse and judgment that would befall the unbeliever and the undevoted to the Lord. The word Maranatha was an "exclamation of approaching divine judgment" (blueletterbible.org). However, it was also an expression of encouragement to the believer. In the days of Roman rule, the government under which Paul wrote his letters to the Corinthians and the other early churches, it was a dangerous time for believers. People were expected to declare that Caesar was lord, and if they did not, they would be persecuted, tortured and killed. Christians would comfort each other with one word, which was used as a greeting much like the word shalom in Jewish culture (Chuck Smith's notes on 1 Cor. 16:22).

The word Maranatha served as a constant reminder that the Lord is coming! Imagine how powerful that one word would have been to encourage the persecuted Christians. No matter what you face, Jesus is coming! Be careful not to focus on material things because Jesus is coming! Strive to keep your eyes on what pleases the Lord because Jesus is coming! It was a word of hope, a directive to

"He which testified these things saith, Surely I come quickly. Amen. Even so, come, Lord Jesus."

With that final word, let Maranatha be your reminder for joy, comfort and hope today!

With love in Christ,

Dolly.

⌘ Power Confession ⌘

I am an overcomer through the armor of God.

Put on the whole armor of God, that you may be able to stand against the wiles of the devil.

Ephesians 6:11

hardworking farmer should be the first to receive a share of the crops. Reflect on what I am saying, for the Lord will give you insight into all this.

2 Timothy 2:1-7

In this passage we have an interesting list of people that seem to have no real connection with each other. I love how the Word puts us in the place where we are made to look at the qualities that we might not see in any other way. Let's look at the people:

1. Soldier

2. Athlete

3. Farmer

What are the qualities that make each of these folks effective in their roles? Let's look at each one individually and see how we, too, can have these qualities that will make us who we need to be in the Kingdom.

or loser, but that the important thing is to follow the rules.

You can get all the way to the end, but even if you are the winner, if you have not followed the instructions, you will be disqualified.

Are you disqualified from the race because you are doing it your way instead of God's way? Sometimes we are focused on the wrong things. We are focused on the end and not how we got there. God wants us to pay attention to the details that will help us run the race with integrity.

3. Farmer

Verse 6 mentions the farmer. The Word says that he is hardworking. This is an important quality in service to the Lord. Laziness is not a characteristic that can be tolerated in the Kingdom.

When God comes for us, what will He find you doing? Will you be busy or sleeping? Think about other farmer qualities:

Patience, the quality of waiting ... waiting on the Lord. You can't plant today and eat tomorrow.

Unbothered

RACHEL CHIMA – HOUSTON, TEXAS

It was another Saturday for the Chima Tribe. I sat in my study with a steaming cup of coffee in my favorite Mickey Mouse mug, savoring the taste of peanut butter smeared graham crackers and meticulously sliced bananas. I could hear my four rambunctious children, each over talking the next in a passionate discussion over what's for dinner.

I glanced down at my phone to see a text from my sister, empathically asking if I would like to escape to her room. I smiled. It was at this moment that I unexplainably realized that I was "unbothered."

to go from increase to scarcity.

This was seen during the time of great harvest amongst the Moabites when Bethlehem was experiencing famine. They both knew what devastation and grief felt like when they both lost their husbands and were left to fend for themselves. Naomi and Ruth understood how it felt to be the topic of conversation and the reception of sympathetic glances.

It's in their stories that we see how God was working behind the scenes to take them from a barren life to a blessed life. We witness this in the redemptive love and provision of their kinsman, Boaz. Like a good book, we didn't see this coming, but what hope it brings to our personal circumstances!

God desires to exchange the areas of our life that seem barren with blessings of His Redemption and the fullness of His unequivocal love. Hope! Just as He took their pain and produced purpose, He desires to wipe every tear, heal every hurt and strengthen our weary souls. He wants to exchange our story for His glory.

Together, we must choose to be "unbothered" as

Power Confession

I am surrounded by Christ, safe from the world.

The thief only comes to steal, kill, and destroy. I came that they may have life, and may have it abundantly.

John 10:10

about a person thinking you were sending it to another person, but instead sent it to the person the text was about? I am definitely guilty of this! I have too many times fallen victim to the lie that I can do multiple things at once and have unfortunately spoiled plans, upset someone, and deeply confused others while learning that my fingers can be faster than my brain.

It doesn't just happen with texting, though. Often, we speak without realizing what is coming out of our mouth, and we react without fully processing what is being said to us. We may jump to unnecessary conclusions, get preliminarily defensive, or mentally move the conversation along prematurely. Our brains are these amazing and wonderful things, but how fast they send messages to the rest of our body is shocking and an area where we need the Holy Spirit. We need the Holy Spirit to slow down and filter our actions and emotions, helping us to avoid harmful miscommunication.

Being emotional beings is such a beautiful thing. We have the ability to feel things deeply, especially women. Our emotional depth and complexity allow opportunity to speak without selfishly thinking about what we have to add to the conversation.

Slow to Speak

Slowing our response allows us to process what we are being told and formulate the proper response. This gives the Holy Spirit a chance to filter what we are saying and helps us to make sure we are responding in a godly manner and not in a selfish way. Being slow to speak allows us to think before we speak and not the other way around, which tends to get us in trouble. Speaking is not just our verbal communication, but how we respond to emails, Facebook posts, texts, etc. Proper tone is not always conveyed through text. Giving ourselves a chance to think about the person, remind ourselves who we are talking to, and picture how the conversation would sound if we were in person helps us to avoid miscommunication.

Slow to Become Angry

Now, we get to the emotional response. Personally, I fight getting angry when I see someone

Fear and Anxiety

BOBBIE GARCIA – HALLETTSVILLE, TEXAS

There is no fear in love. But perfect love
drives out fear, because fear has to do with
punishment. The one who fears is not made
perfect in love.

1 John 4:18

Whether we like to admit it or not, anxiety's roots can be found in a lack of trust in God's goodness.

If we retrace our steps when we start to experience fear, we can find the thoughts and beliefs that have preceded it. These can be thoughts of some-to say, "Did God really say—"

Let this be your prayer and declaration today to combat anxiety:

Father, I know you want good things for me and You give good gifts to Your children who ask. You love me with a perfect love and even those things that do not seem good have to work out for my good. I believe what You say and will not let my own thoughts exalt themselves over Your Word and all that You say You are.

Power Confession

My despair is vanquished through the love of Christ.

[Cast] all your worries on him, because he cares for you.

1 Peter 5:7

Our Heart His Mission

HE IS THERE ALL THE TIME!

He is our constant help in time of need. You are never alone and never in need, because He always provides.

- Even when you can't see it through those long chapters ... He is there setting it all up!
- When you don't have the resources ... He is there preparing!
- When you feel all alone ... He is there beside you!
- When you can't face another day ... He is there to hold you!
- When there are no answers for your questions ... HE IS THE ANSWER!

We serve a mighty, all-powerful, all-knowing God, and He is faithful! Turn your eyes away from the events of your life and to the Author of your life. It will change your perspective!

Teach me, LORD, the way of your decrees,

Rise Up, Momma!

LAURA YARBROUGH – NEW CANEY, TEXAS

What happens when women decide to walk in the power given to them by their Maker? Rachel gave birth to the child who saved Israel from starvation. Rahab saved God's plan for a promised land. Ruth served as an example of the blessing of faithfulness. Mary became the mother to her Lord and Savior. If you and I will rise to the challenge like those women, we can be a link in the chain that draws all men and women to God.

Deborah, revealed in Judges 4 and 5, was just such a link. When it comes to great women of the Bible, Deborah is among the most influential. She is

When she gets to verse 7, my heart does a little dance, because that verse seems so relevant to me and the life I live. It hits me right smack dab in the middle of my everything.

"Village life ceased. It ceased until I,
Deborah, arose; I arose like a mother in
Israel."

Judges 5:7

Deborah didn't wait for someone else to do it. She saw that life as she knew it had stopped; so what did she do? She arose. She stood up and did what needed to be done. What did she compare her rise to? Did she rise like the powerful judge of Israel that she had become? Did she rise like a warrior whose army refused to fight unless she led them? No. She compared herself to the most fundamental, accessible element of her being—a mother.

"I arose like a mother in Israel."

Power Confession

I can surmount every wall and conquer every obstruction.

No temptation has taken you except what is common to man. God is faithful, who will not allow you to be tempted above what you are able, but will with the temptation also make the way of escape, that you may be able to endure it.

1 Corinthians 10:13

strengthen us in the healthiest ways, or it can destroy us.

It is interesting to see the synonyms listed in the thesaurus for "comparison" and "'encouragement."

COMPARISON

contrast, judgment, assessment, evaluation, appraisal

None of which sound like happy words. I feel exhausted even thinking about the various applications here.

I once heard Kari Jobe say in an interview, "Comparison will be the number one thing that will keep you from doing what God's calling you to do. He's put a gift and a call and desire in your heart that is different than anyone else's. And you're wired that way for a reason."

You see, you are invaluable, irreplaceable and incomparable. The life you've lived, the lessons taught and learned, the people you have impacted, the way your mind thinks differently than anyone

---

❧ Power Confession ❧

I am enriched with joy through the power of Christ.

For my yoke is easy, and my burden is light.

Matthew 11:30

days and weeks, the Master Gardener noticed the crack becoming wider and wider. Upon closer inspection, he saw within the darkness of that crack a frail, green stem silently pushing its way toward the sunlight. What a day of celebration it was when after weeks of careful watching, the Master Gardener saw that the culprit behind that now large crack was a tiny plant with two new leaves. He noticed how proud the aggressive seedling looked as it quietly yet securely made its way out of the darkness and into the sunlight above the broken stone in the walkway.

"That stone walkway was definitely no match for this determined little plant," thought the Gardener.

By summer's end, a beautiful bloom had appeared on the top of the long slender plant. It was a bright yellow blossom that seemed to announce to everyone that passed by, "Look, Master Gardener, I made it!"

Sometimes, situations in our lives can seem hopeless, as if there is no way out. When you begin to feel that way, remember this story about the little plant that struggled hard to make its way to the surface. You will begin to see cracks in that ho-hum existence and a way out of it that you had never thought of before. With time, you too will burst out into the sunlight, a brilliant testimony of the Master Gardener's work.

Power Confession

I am strong in battle, and all my enemies are overthrown.

But if you will go, take action, be strong for the battle. God will overthrow you before the enemy; for God has power to help, and to overthrow.

2 Chronicles 25:8

street from our ministry center, in a broken-down house that looked like a single garage. There were old mattresses piled high in front and there was junk sitting all around. Every day she could be seen walking the streets with her "borrowed" HEB shopping cart … looking to collect whatever "treasure" she could find. She would come to our Hope Pantry, pushing her way to sit in the very front, her phone stuffed in her bra with her hair shaved like a man's and growing straight up. She was the roughest, toughest rattlesnake that we'd ever seen in Texas! I'm telling you that she could swear more than any Marine I have ever heard! We even heard her swearing and yelling at the drug lord across the street one day … we were so worried she would get shot, but she didn't care! Carmen ruled those streets, day and night!

Carmen would sit there in the very front during our Pantry service and ask for extra tacos … demanding more, actually. Sometimes our volunteers were scared and would avoid her. The people sitting around her would roll their eyes whenever she spoke. No one wanted to sit by her, for fear of running to our door just as I was walking out. She said, "Please, come. The police are at Carmen's house, and she's not answering." We went to her home and found her neighbors standing there. We gathered them together and prayed while the police entered and found her dead. There may have not been any tears shed that day by them but I did, and we realized that she had left her mark on that neighborhood and us.

Carmen's one desire was to have her son stop the drugs, and her prayers were answered that day. Her son met us at the funeral and told us that when she passed on, he was in jail and received Christ as his Savior! I know the angels were rejoicing the day she arrived in heaven, and she is walking on the streets of gold today ... no more "borrowed" carts to push looking for treasures, because she has found the treasure of eternal life.

Jesus loves us all, no matter who we are, and He calls on us to love the unloved. Carmen was one of the unloved ... and believe me she didn't make it easy to love her. But Christ loved her and asked me to love her, too.

❦ Power Confession ❧

I am a mighty warrior for God.

Be strong and courageous. Don't be afraid or scared of them; for Yahweh your God himself is who goes with you. He will not fail you nor forsake you.

Deuteronomy 31:6

and the scorching hot summer seasons will not last forever. There will be times of refreshing.

When the harder seasons of life seem to last much longer than we anticipated, weariness can easily set in. Anxious thoughts can rush through our minds and we wonder how we will make it until the time of refreshing finally arrives.

It's during the "in-between times" that we struggle. As women with many responsibilities, we must keep doing life. But how is this done, especially during the in-between times?

2 Peter 1:3 tells us that we have EVERYTHING we need for life and godliness. If you notice, it did not say we have some things—it says we have absolutely everything we need for life. The word life in this Scripture means the absolute fullness of life. A real and genuine life that is not only active, but is filled with energy, effort, enthusiasm, physical strength, and good health. A life that trusts Christ and is devoted to God.

You might say, "This sounds great, but this is not my reality during this in-between time."

I hear you and I empathize with you.

need to function, thrive, and overcome during your in-between season. You can trust in God's promise that He will never fail you, nor abandon you.

A prayer of submission:

Lord, it's me.

You see me and you know exactly where I am. I ask for your supernatural strength today. Please breathe the breath of life into me and restore my soul. I know that you have gone before me and that you are leading me step by step. This is a hard place to be. Nevertheless, I submit my will to your will. I know that you see what I cannot see and that you have my best interests in mind. God, you are faithful. I know that this too shall pass. I will continue to trust you in this season of my life. I will follow you and I will not look back. Thank you for truly being the LORD of my life.

In Jesus' Name, Amen.

It's Time to Move

STEPHANIE KELLER – LA PORTE, TEXAS

The book of Genesis ends with the glorious salvation of God's people when they moved to Egypt to escape the famine where God had worked to place an Israelite in leadership giving the Jews a place of honor in a foreign land. But Egypt was not the promise. When we open up the book of Exodus, it begins with letting us know there is a new ruler in Egypt who didn't know anything about the honor of the Jews. He didn't know about the man God sent to save Egypt and make it a great nation. All he saw when he looked at the people of God was fear. They had become so great in number that he feared an

Egypt by God's design.

But, by the end of the chapter, we see Moses fleeing for his life out of Egypt, away from both the palace and the slave camp. No one wanted him, not even his own people.

I've been recently reminded of childbirth. I'm a few years (or 12) removed from the experience, and in all the joys and love in parenthood, it's easy to forget the pain of that time. But ... ask any mom about her birth experience, and she can recall it well.

My last pregnancy was twins, and I remember comparing it to my singleton and how much more difficult it was. I have often jokingly said that I am allergic to pregnancy because I was so sick for the entire time with both pregnancies. I had terrible "all-day sickness" because mine did not just strike in the mornings. While carrying my twins I was hospitalized multiple times for severe dehydration, malnutrition and early labor. I was ordered to lie on my back for long stretches (days and weeks) and to not walk unless I was heading to and from the restroom. An accurate description would be intensely uncomfortable.

would they ever leave their comfortable lifestyle unless something made them uncomfortable? God never intended His people to live as honored foreigners. He had a land He wanted them to possess as their own nation, to live honored among nations in their own right, no longer visitors but kings.

You may be mourning the loss of a position in life. You feel you've lost the comfort you were accustomed to; the security you loved. I understand. The comfort you've lived in and loved seemed suddenly yanked from under you, and now you've found yourself no longer an honored guest but a slave to your situation—or like Moses, chased out by those who claimed to love you.

You might be crying out to God, "But YOU brought me here! This was YOUR will!"

You say, "Why is the good life I once lived now over?"

It was part of your journey, not your promised land. It is never God's will or plan for us to become comfortable in the desert and stay in tents all our lives. Our stops along life's journey have a purpose, but they aren't the destination, and if He never

I won't tell you my story in detail; but I will share that I was made uncomfortable and forced to move because God had better and more planned for me.

God has more and better planned for each of us, but we have to move. Change is uncomfortable, and we may HATE it, but do we trust God? Don't stop and set up camp in the wilderness. Don't stay in Egypt as an honored guest, all the while slowly descending into slavery. Don't get so angry at the discomfort, the pain, the mourning, that in your anger, you stomp your feet and stubbornly refuse to move. Don't refuse to leave the slavery because you're angry that you are no longer an honored foreigner.

A sure sign of someone who is STUCK is: "It should have been ..." or, "We've never done it that way before ..."

MOVE! Trust God and MOVE!

Move into a new season. Move into a new job. Move into forgiveness. Move into a new time and position in life. Stop looking back and move.

Grace That Is Amazing

BETH A. WIEHE – HOUSTON, TEXAS

And God is able to make all grace abound to you, so that having all sufficiency in all things at all times, you may abound in every good work.

2 Corinthians 9:8 (ESV)

The power of God when manifested through His grace at work in a believer's life becomes a powerful and vivid display of His love toward humanity. God's *abundance* and our *human emptiness* are a perfect match.

that God has stamped on their life at birth or conception.

I think of our purpose or destiny as the void that waits to be fulfilled through God's grace within us. He desires for us to yield our lives to Him so that His strength can fill that "capacity" (or void) that we all have in us.

In God's plan, each person has been given something to do that shows who He is. We seek Him to get clarity on what that is and then take our place in the body of Christ and bear fruit.

Grace is WHAT GOD GIVES BELIEVERS as they surrender their lives to Him daily. His portion of grace is sufficient for each day so that we may accomplish His will.

God's grace gives us confidence in His great love, a love that is undeserved. We need only to reach out to accept His love though His eternal grace. It is a gift we can never earn, and yet it is something God desires all men to receive. He lavishes it on us.

Paul was the most undeserving man (by human discernment), yet God chose to pursue him and pour out His grace on him. God desired Paul to receive *glory and excellence.*

2 Peter 1:3 (ESV)

God's grace is the "enough" that we need to walk through the difficult seasons or circumstances of life. His divine grace equips us to see ourselves as we are in His presence and helps our perception of ourselves to be in line with what He sees.

His grace is what helps us to stay focused on the truth and to not be swayed by what surrounds us.

Among alumni from my university, a man my husband and I knew married a fine Christian young woman who had grown up attending AG Tabernacle in Houston, only to lose his wife six months later in a car accident. He was so severely injured he couldn't attend her funeral. Even in his devastating sorrow, God's grace covered him, filling him with a strength that was not natural but supernatural. God gave me a glimpse of true grace watching what that young man went through and the faith he exhibited in the continued goodness of God.

Grace is what God provides when life is more

Our Heart His Mission

This is Amazing Grace, by Phil Wickham
He Will Hold Me Fast, by Keith and Krystin Getty

I pray that your lives will reflect more and more of His grace. In faith. In service. In His gifting and call on your life.

Power Confession

I am filled with mercy and grace in my time of need.

Let us therefore draw near with boldness to the throne of grace, that we may receive mercy, and may find grace for help in time of need.

Hebrews 4:16

While doing so, I had to cradle the jacket in my arms. Embrace it. Hug it almost.

I began to think, how many of us are hurting, suffering, broken, worn out, exhausted? I envisioned us holding on ...

... by our last nerve,

... our last hope,

... our last thread.

All the while, the Father is beckoning us to let go and just be held. It's in His embrace where we find peace and healing and begin growing again as He repositions us securely in His will.

The lyrics of *Just Be Held*, by Casting Crowns, began to ring over and over in my mind.

The words speak of being on our knees, and our answers feeling farther away than we can imagine.

God says, "I've got you. I'm holding you. You don't have to keep trying so hard."

He tells us our world is falling into place, not apart. He is still on the throne, and He is in control.

So, let go, and just be held.

Even to your old age and gray hairs I am He,

Scripture Index